Once upon a time there was a very ordinary girl.
One day she heard a knock at the door.

It was the world asking her for help.

THE DONKEY'S TALE

Margaret Gray

Regal Books

A Division of GL Publications
Ventura, CA U.S.A.

North American Edition Including Canada
Published by Regal Books
A Division of GL Publications
Ventura, California, U.S.A.

Printed by LEGO, Vicenza, Italy.
Co-edition arranged by Angus Hudson, London.

ISBN 0-8307-0963-0
5111209

'Why me?' she asked.

'What can I do to help?

'Why not someone with more sense who is more reliable?
I always make mistakes.

'Or someone who knows what to say?
When I want to say what I feel...

'hundreds of words race to the edge of my mouth fighting to be the first to come out and they all get mixed up.

'Or why not one of those people who are brilliant at everything?

'Or at least someone less afraid?

'I'm just useless!'

'You too?' said a donkey.

'Just look at me,' he said, 'I've got long funny ears,...

'my legs are too short...

'and I'm often stubborn and moody.

'But a long time ago...

'in a faraway land...

' a man chose me.

'Not a dashing white horse, but funny old me.

'He was heavy and the road was long, but he always gave me the strength to get there.

'You see, when a racehorse runs fast, no one is surprised...

'When a beautiful beast is graceful, people accept it as natural...

'And no one is startled when a carthorse is strong.

'But when people saw me carrying this man and I wasn't clumsy
and I didn't kick or grumble...

'They were seeing a miracle—something happening that was bigger than me.

'He doesn't need another genius—he needs a few donkeys who know they have to
depend on his strength—not theirs
        his wisdom—not theirs
           his words—not theirs.'

'So it doesn't matter that I feel useless,' said the girl. 'He will show me what to do and will give me what I need to do it.'

'Yes,' said the donkey, 'And the other thing about being a donkey is, every now and then ...

'to stand in front of a mirror...

'and have a good laugh!'

The Story of the Donkey

As they approached Jerusalem, near the towns of Bethphage and Bethany, they came to the Mount of Olives. Jesus sent two of his disciples on ahead with these instructions: 'Go to the village there ahead of you. As soon as you get there, you will find a colt tied up that has never been ridden. Untie it and bring it here. And if someone asks you why you are doing that, tell him that the Master needs it and will send it back at once.'

So they went and found a colt out in the street, tied to the door of a house. As they were untying it, some of the bystanders asked them, 'What are you doing, untying that colt?'

They answered just as Jesus had told them, and the men let them go. They brought the colt to Jesus, threw their cloaks over the animal, and Jesus got on. Many people spread their cloaks on the road, while others cut branches in the fields and spread them on the road. The people who were in front and those who followed behind began to shout, 'Praise God! God bless him who comes in the name of the Lord! God bless the coming kingdom of King David, our father! Praise God!'

The Gospel of Mark
chapter 11, verses 1 to 10.

From the Good News Bible—New Testament Copyright
© American Bible Society 1966, 1971, 1976